The Haidas

Original Notebook and Sketches

by

George Mercer Dawson

1878

Cover: George Mercer Dawson's map based on his 1878 survey of the Queen Charlotte Islands. Geological Survey of Canada, Multicoloured Geological Map 139, 1878.

Legend:
Dark green: Miocene
Light green: Cretaceous
Light beige: Agglomerates, Ash Rocks probably Triassic
Dark beige: Triassic
Red: Intrusive Granite, Diorite etc.

https://open.library.ubc.ca/viewer/bcbooks/1.0222501#p28 8z-7r0f:map%20139

"Not the least curious of the customs of the Haidas, and probably with some religious significance, are those connected with dancing ceremonies. It is remarkable too that most of these are said to have been derived from the Tshimsians of the neighbouring mainland, a people speaking a language quite distinct and who [had been] at bitter war with the Haidas."

— George M. Dawson
page 15 of the manuscript

Introduction

"I present a few details concerning the remarkable race of people living on the islands, about whom, though perhaps one of the most interesting native peoples of America, very little accurate information has yet been published."

— George M. Dawson
Page 2 of the manuscript

This notebook by George Mercer Dawson (GMD) 1849-1901, was originally imaged by McGill University Archives for the Dawson-Harrington fonds. In this booklet, to ensure the best legibility, each page of the notebook is spread horizontally across two pages.

"The Haidas" [modern plural "Haida"] is an 1878 essay including his own pencilled edits and comments. Much of it was then prepared for *Harper's New Monthly Magazine* who published it in 1880 — but a good 30% of this handwritten manuscript is unique and never before published. The pencilled marginalia by Dawson show his pre-publication edits including crossed-out parts, and long vertical lines indicating parts that were not to be included. Overall it also formed part of his thinking in compiling Appendix A and B of his 1880 *Report on the Queen Charlotte Islands* published by the Geological Survey of Canada (GSC). See References.

From 1875-1898, largely not in winter, he explored western Canada including the northwest coast of British Columbia including the Queen Charlotte Islands (Haida Gwaii). "The object of our [1878] expedition was to carry out a preliminary geological, geographical and general exploration of the islands, in connection with the Geological Survey of Canada." (page 2 of ms) of which he was Assistant Director (1883-) and Director (1895-1901).

He was personally interested in the ethnographic study of the "vanishing Indian" community, its culture and language. He would often be writing long into the night on the subject (he was a bit bookish). Raised in upper-class Victorian Montreal (his father Sir William was principal of McGill University) he was well educated, had excellent writing skills, and was good at sketching and watercolours. I have included sketches from another of his 1878 notebooks, the year he was surveying the Queen Charlotte Islands, although these were not part of "The Haidas" notebook per se.

Since he had a humpback, native peoples may have considered him 'of the spirit' and many may have respected him and let him into their midst.

"To many he was affectionately called the 'The Little Giant' and, to the First Nations People of Canada, 'Skookum Tumtum' meaning 'brave, cheery man'...His report **Sketches of the Past and Present condition of the Indians of Canada** *was particularly historically and culturally important in the early development understanding and respect for Canada's First Nations Peoples."* See https://archive.org/details/cihm_02365/page/n5/mode/2up
— John Ashton, *Saltwire*, *New Glasgow News*, Nova Scotia, Sept 25, 2017.

"It was in British Columbia that Dawson earned his reputation as 'one of Canada's foremost contributors to ethnology' and as a 'father of Canadian anthropology'...As an artist and poet, he was captivated by the beauty of the Haida totem-poles and by the intelligence and skills reflected in the construction of their villages. As a Darwinian scientist, he perceived a highly evolved culture...Dawson's pioneering research and dedication focused international attention on Canada's rich ethnological heritage...and deeply influenced the theoretical and institutional development of anthropology in this country."
— Suzanne Zeller and Gale Avrith-Wakeam *Dictionary of Canadian Biography* Vol. XIII.

Sketches by GMD of Haida Gwaii in 1878

Not included in "The Haidas" essay, these pages are from a separate Dawson notebook during his 1878 survey of the Queen Charlotte Islands.
Source: https://digitalarchives.library.mcgill.ca /MUA/MG1022/mua_george-mercer-dawson-diary_1878 _envelope-49_MG1022.pdf

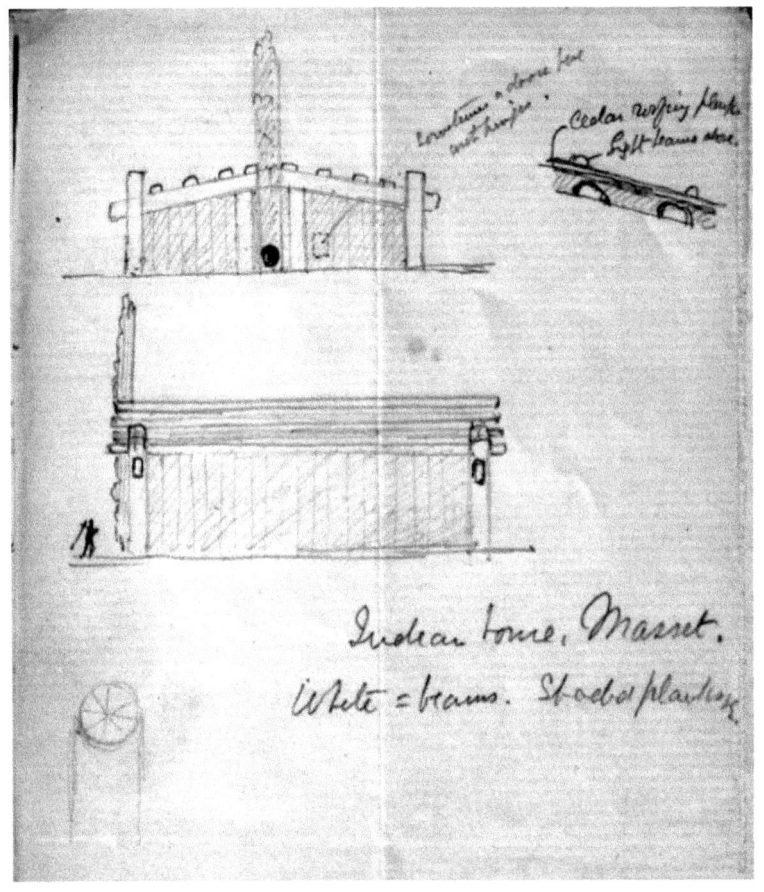

Sketches by George Mercer Dawson, Queen Charlotte Islands, 1878. McGill University mg1022 file 134 page 5.

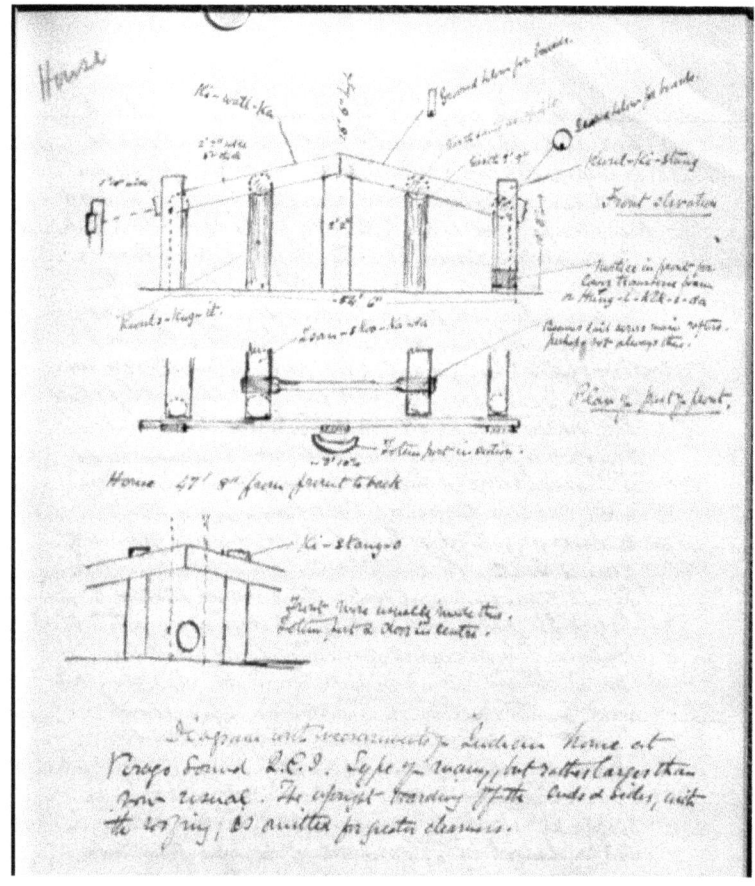

Text and sketch by George Mercer Dawson, Queen Charlotte Islands, 1878. McGill University mg1022 file 134 page 192

Sketches by George Mercer Dawson, Queen Charlotte Islands, 1878. McGill University mg1022 file 134 page 157.

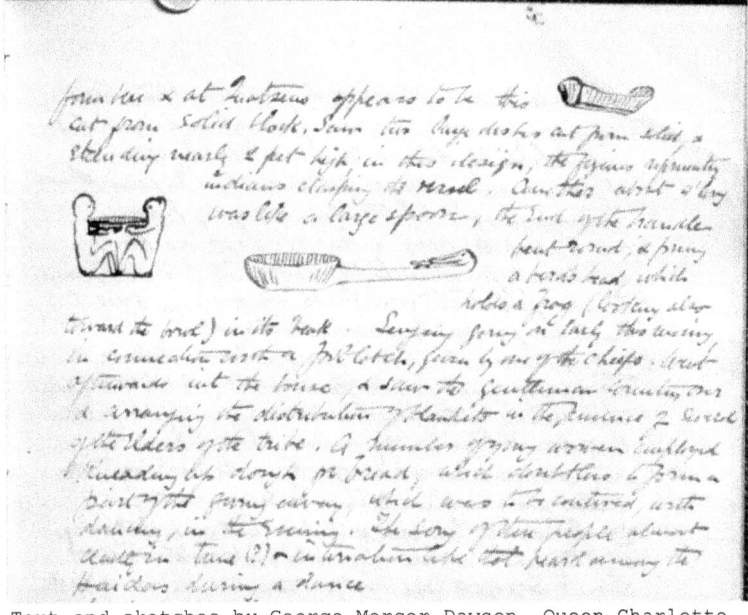

Text and sketch by George Mercer Dawson, Queen Charlotte
Islands, 1878. McGill University mg1022 file 134 page 198

Text and sketches by George Mercer Dawson, Queen Charlotte
Islands, 1878. McGill University mg1022 file 134 page 215

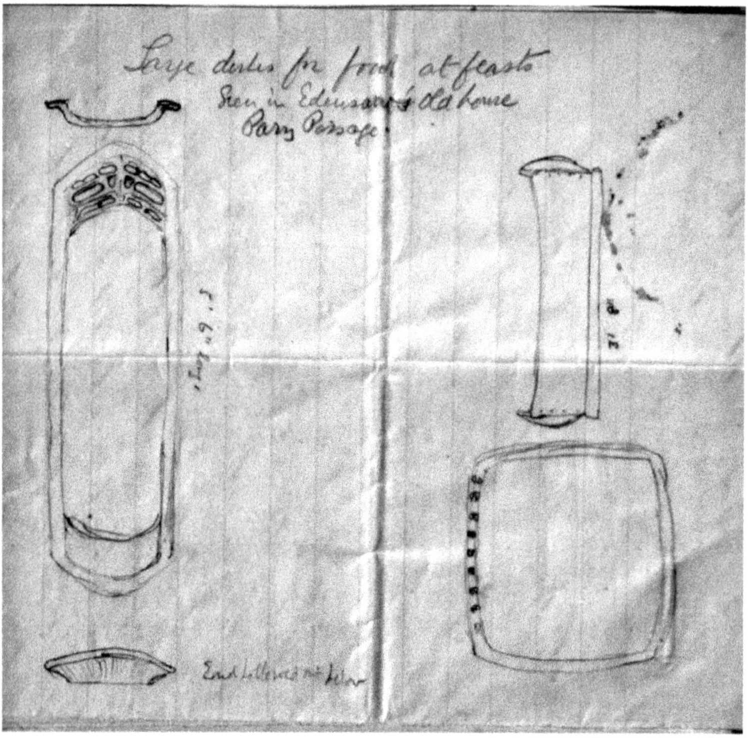

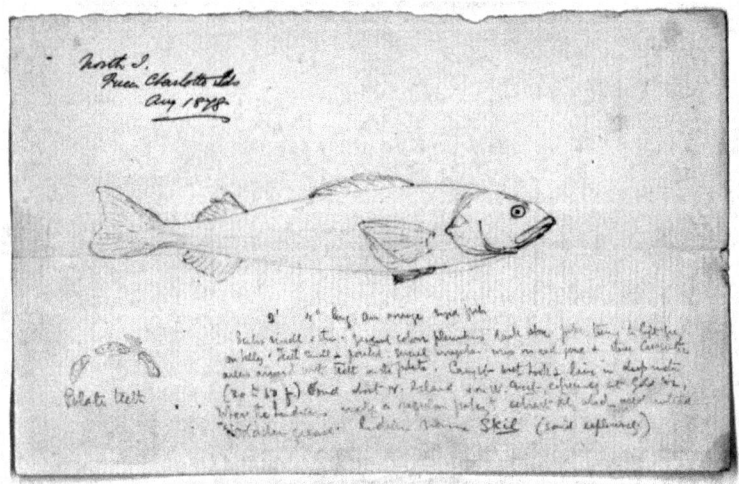

Sketches by George Mercer Dawson, Queen Charlotte Islands, 1878. McGill University mg1022 file 134 page 3

Sketch by George Mercer Dawson, Queen Charlotte Islands, 1878. McGill University mg1022 file 51 page 15

The Haidas

Handwritten 1878 notebook

by George Mercer Dawson

original, complete and unabridged

The Haidas

Leaving Victoria, Vancouver Island on the 27th of July 1878, in the little Schooner Wanderer of twenty tons burden, we steered north-westward for the Queen Charlotte Islands; a journey as England — sufficiently trying for the English into County of Vancouver Island, exposed to the full sweep of the Great North Pacific, we were obliged to navigate the inner channels & wonderful series of winding fiords which characterize the coast of British Columbia & identify among its half-submerged mountain ranges. Channels like these woven well adapted for steam navigation, & wonderfully picturesque & grand though they are, are tedious enough for sailing vessels.

... they are, an tedious enough for sailing vessels. It would however either divide up or down the channel, shutting off its mountain walls, & what with calms, & the rapids & constantly changing tidal current, we spent many a weary hour at anchor, or even retrogressing. Sixteen days thus slowly passing brought us to Milbank Sound, whence, abandoning the idea of visiting first the North end of the islands, we lay across for their southern extremity. In making the traverse of eighty miles we were first becalmed

& then, without some discomfort & danger, ... half a gale from the North Westward, & on the 12th of June completed our voyage, made for hundred miles, by casting anchor between the island wooded shores of a cove in Clmeaset Channel, which separates Revost & Moresby Islands.

In April - Your expedition was to carry out a
Preliminary Geological geographical & general
exploration of the Islands, in connection with the
Geological Survey of Canada, & in this work we
were engaged till the Autumn storms warned us
again to seek a more southern latitude. We were
furnished, besides provisions for the Seamen, with
drags & appliances for procuring Specimens,
photographic apparatus & meteorological & other
apparatus, and which we were kept busy enough
during the season. For the results obtained of these,
& with the Seamen & Cruyfoos among the rocks
I do not propose intend to refer any further, but to
present a few details concerning the circumstance

presents few details concerning the unsearchable race of people living on the islands, about whom, though perhaps one of the most interesting native peoples of America, so little accurate information has yet been furnished.

Within the limits of the Province of British Columbia, in the absence of a trustworthy Census, the native races, or Indians, are roughly estimated to number 30,000. Tribes associated by language, & collectively belonging to the great Tinneh family, inhabit the whole northern interior of the country. Forming true ... or the south, & occupying the southern part of the interior are Indians of the Salish Connection, divided into many tribes, having different names, but all allied in language. The differences between the dialects being generally not so great as to prevent intercommunication. Along the

Coast, & on the outlying islands are scattered a great number of tribes, differing markedly, &, in former years frequently hostile one to another. In certain modes of life & thought, there is complete diversity between the Coast Indians & those of the interior, a diversity which practically transcends the racial divisions.

Of the Northern interior, the Indians inhabiting a country for the most part thinly wooded, still remain as they have been heretofore, hunters & fishers, but in many places they now also cultivate small garden patches, where they grow such vegetables as require little attention. For their winter food supply they generally depend chiefly on fish which is dried & cured during the summer. On all the tributaries of the

during the Summer. Or all the [totatoris] of the
Fraser Salmon is taken, plus in great abundance;
of these tribes were the Coast [...] succeeded
in maintaining against the Coast Indians the
control of some party the various dwellers living on
which Salmon can be caught. Hitherto they made an
annual migration, which they look upon as a sort
of holiday making, Wealthy during the Season in
abundance of fresh fish, & on their return carrying
back with them a supply for the cold months.

At the Southern Portion of the interior, the Washroo has
come much more freely in contact with the whites
& broad[...] made material progress. In the
early days of gold mining labour was in great
demand, & consequently Indian who could
or would work was employed at good wages from

of British Columbia

Skidaa's Travels to Casting Peoples

Of the tribes inhabiting the coast, the Haidas are in many respects the most interesting. The Queen Charlotte Islands, which they inhabit (as separated by wide water traps took from the Archipelago forming the country, the mainland of British Columbia, to the South-east, & from the Southern extremity of Alaska to the North. They form a compact group, & it is perhaps to their compactness, isolation & homogeneity that we owe the fact that the Haidas while remarkably distinct from mainland tribes of the coast, are in language & customs so nearly the same in all parts of their own territory. The extreme length of the Queen Charlotte Islands is one hundred & eighty miles, with a greatest breadth of sixty miles.

During Captain Cooks' last voyage in the Pacific
it was discovered that a lucrative trade in furs
might be opened between the North-western Coast of
America & China, & though the existence of a party of
the Queen Charlotte Islands had been known to
the Spaniards since the voyage of Juan Perez,
despatched by the Viceroy of Mexico in 1774, it is
to the traders who followed in the track of Cook that
we owe [most] of the fuller discoveries on the front
of the coast of it. is they who appear to have first
come in contact with the Haidas. During the
[opening] & during the [earlier] years of the present
century the Queen Charlotte Islands were not
infrequently visited by trading vessels. The sea-
otter, however, — the chief fur was the [most]

Polar, towers) — The Esquimaux was the most
valuable articles of trade, America & the islanders —
being known by scarce through continuous
hunting for many years But were careless how
called obtained of the provision many years back.
The islands on which ... on, to, on, ... side of the
Tropic & the southern part of British Columbia,
which of late years has assumed considerable
proportions.

The earliest ... of the Hebrides which I have seen
able to ... is that given in Captain Dixon's
narrative & bears date July 1787. Brian Point
made the land & the islands bear their North-
western extremity in the vicinity of Port ... island.)

The ... : ✳   ✳ At noon we saw a deep bay which

✳ : A voyage round the World, but more particularly to the
North-west coast of North America. London 1789

[left margin note:]
& given in the narrative
of his voyage a detailed
account of his meeting &
intercourse with the natives
of his time and their fur
furs.

GMD 21

bore North East ½ East — x x We were determining
to make it — if possible as there was every probability
of meeting with inhabitants. During the night we
had light variable winds in every direction, together
with a heavy swell from the South West. So that in
the morning of the second we found our Utmost effort
to reach the bay ineffectual. However, a moderate
breeze springing up at North East, we stood in for
the land. Close by the wind, with our starboard tacks
on board. At eleven o'clock, to our very great joy,
we saw several canoes full of Indians who
appeared to have been out at sea, making towards
us. On their coming up with the vessel we found
them to be a fishing party, but none of them were
excellent trim craft. They did not seem, however,

us. On their coming up with the Vessel we found them to be a fishing party, but four of them were excellent rowers. The air however, inclined to inspire of true — though we endeavoring to tempt them by exhibiting various articles of trade, such as toes, hatchets, adzes, towels, tin-kettles, pans &c, their attention seemed chiefly taken up with viewing the Vessel, which they apparently did not think of wonder & surprise. This was looked on as a good omen, & the event showed that for once we were not mistaken. After their curiosity in some measure subsided, they began to trade, & we presently taught what species of clocks they had got, in exchange for toes, which they seemed to like very much. They made signs for us to go in towards the shore, & gave us to understand that we should find there inhabitants & plenty of furs. By ten o'clock

we were within a mile of the shore, & saw the
village where the pelicans should right-a-breast
grus; it consisting of about six huts which
appeared to be built in a more regular form than
any we had yet seen, & the situation very pleasant
but the shore was rocky, & afforded no place for
us to anchor in. x x Leaving this two several

the people whom we traded took in the mornings
had been on shore, probably to show their trade
acquiring bargains, but on seeing us start for
the bay, they presently hauled off after us, & joined
by several other canoes.x x & seen now commenced
which absolutely peppers all description, & with
which we were to overjoyed that we could scarcely
believe the evidence of our senses. there were two

believe the evidence of our senses. There were ten
Canoes about the Ships, which contained as
nearly as I could estimate one hundred &
twenty people; many of these wrought-most
beautiful brown cloaks, others excellent fishing!
& in short, some came simply handed, & the
sophistry with which they told them was a
circumstance additionally pleasing; they
giving guarantee into each other about what I would
sell his cloak first; & some actually threw their
furs on board, if anybody was at hand to
receive them, but the little particular care that some
got from the vessel unpaid. x x In less than
half an hour we purchased near three hundred
Cloaks &c.; an excellent quality, a circumstance
which greatly raised our spirits!!

✳ Though often called beaver skins, as is the place in

fact our manufacture, the furs obtained were really sea-otter

skins, as appears by other evidence. The skins purchased

during this voyage, estimated at the prices then ruling at

Canton must have been worth about $90,000

Captain Douglas, or Meares who is

on of the best known of the fur trading voyagers on this coast,

visited the Sirene Party the Islando in a few years

later, & gives an interesting account of his dealings

with the natives which is known to legendary pr-

inportion here. He is mentioned because on visiting

the present Chief of that region, Edensaw, for the

name of the first white man whom the Haidas had

known he at once for me are Douglas, very well

known' he at once for me Douglas, very well pronounced. On passing him, however, he admitted that Douglas may yet have been absolutely the first, & it is probable to have still earlier navigators that the story of their first knowledge of the White-man procured by the natives before. ——

It was war water, they say, very long ago, when a ship under sail appeared in the vicinity of North Island. The people were all much afraid, the Chief sharing in the general fear but feeling that it was necessary for the sake of his dignity to act a bold part, he armed himself in all the finery used in dancing, went out to sea in his canoe, & prepared a ceremonial dance. It would appear that the childish idea was at first rapidly entertained that the ship was a great kind of some kind, but on approaching it the men on board were seen, & likewise from their dark clothing & the general form & countenance & character of their talk, & things — that indeed sometimes led to about human as they sit bent upon the rocks along the border of the sea. It was noticed that one man would shriek, whereupon all the others would immediately go aloft; till something more being said they would as rapidly descend.

When first visited & whites, the population of the islands probably exceeded 7000, at the present day the number at about 2000, including in this number many who while now living elsewhere on the coast still call the islands their home.

On the coast — still call the islands their home.

On the Southern extremity of the Alaskan Archipelago & adjacent to the Queen Charlotte Islands live the Kai-ga-nai Indians numbering about three hundred & in almost every respect the same with the Haidas. They are in fact merely an offshoot from the main stock, & it is to be remarked that while it might be supposed that tribes of the passage of the Haidas to the Queen Charlotte Islands from the Mainland would be found, it is known by tradition that the Kai-ga-nai took on the contrary migrated to the mainland at a time when doubts of in consequence of intervening wars.

The climate of the Queen Charlotte Islands is exceedingly humid, & they are almost everywhere densely covered with magnificent coniferous trees, mountains 4000 to 5000 feet high rise in their central portion

of these penetrate or all sides of dark deep fiords
with rocky walls. To the northward, it is true, a
wide stretch of low & nearly level country occurs
which may some day support a farming population
but at the present time its sombre woods filled with
dense undergrowth & bristling with prostrate
trunks in every stage of decay, offer little to induce
settlers to locate in or while to penetrate them. The

Haidas therefore, though cultivating here & there along
the shores small potato patches, are essentially
fishermen. Few fields or trails traverse the interior
of the islands, & of these some formerly used when the
population was denser are now abandoned.
The halibut is found in great abundance in the

The halibut is found in great abundance in the
vicinity of the islands, and is more particularly
on those parts West the Haidas depend. These villages
are everywhere situated along the shore, near or where
there [Yukka] banks of the Coast, but always in
proximity to productive halibut banks. Journeys
are made in canoe along the Coast. The Canoes
are chiefly inland from the great Cedar [trees] of
the region which [they] being worked down to a
certain [shape] [thinness], are cleaned, or spread
by the insertion of crosspieces till they are made
to assume a most graceful form, a [few lines]
which would satisfy the most fastidious shipbuilder.
In these larger Canoes the Haidas do undertake
[trade] long voyages on the open sea, a in former
days by their frequent descents on the coast of the
[mainland], of the facility which [attend] they [interested]

Again to their own islands, neither themselves were therefore their any task from Vancouver to Sitka.

In their mode of life & the ingenuity & skill which they display in their manufacture of canoes & other articles, the Haidas do not differ essentially from the other tribes inhabiting the northern part of the coast of British Columbia & Southern Alaska. On the Queen Charlotte Islands, however, the peculiar style of architecture & art elsewhere among the Indians of the North Coast were or are prominently exhibited, phrase certain its greatest development. Whether this way show that the Haidas or their ancestors the into destruction of this is clear, or indicate many that with the greater isolation of the people & consequent increased

isolation of these people & consequent increased
measure of security, the particular idea of the
Indian mind was able to only therefore ———

more fully, we may peer ———. The situation of
the islands & the comparative infrequency with
which they have been visited for many years, have
at least order to preserve intact many features
which have already vanished from the ———
manufactures & ———

As time steals the permanent villages of the Haidas
are invariably situated at the sea shore. They connot
———

several of a single long row of houses with their
running frenzy border between it & the beach or which
the canoes of the tribe (for each village constitutes
a chieftainry) are drawn up. In front of each
house stands a dignified carved post, with
other carved posts, situated irregularly & differing

construction form from these proper to the
bones, are generally removed to the head. Such
a village, seen from a little distance off, the bones
of into grey and the weather, resembles a strip of half
burnt forest - isolated vampires?. The little island
... from the various pits ...
indicate its true character.

Several of the construction of the houses
everywhere using the same ... among the Haidas
They are more substantially framed, & much
more care is given to the fitting together & ornamentation
of the edifice than ... elsewhere seen. The houses are
rectangular, & sometimes over forty feet in length
by side. The walls are formed of planks split

outside. The walls are formed of planks split by
means of wedges from cedar logs & given a
great size. The roof is composed of similar split
planks, on front of slopes down at back side, the
gentle end of the roof — of such an expression
as is allowed — facing the sea, towards which the
door also opens.

The door is usually an oval hole cut in the
base of a protecting carved post — forty to fifty feet
high, which we may call the totem post, but
which the Haidas is known as the *Keehen*. Stooping
to enter one finds that the soil has been excavated
in the interior of the house so as to make the
actual floor sit on eight feet lower than the
surface outside. You descend into it by a few rough
steps, & on looking about above that one or two
large steps run round all four sides of the house.

four ... laid horizontally, with ... supporting
uprights at the ends. They are really levers of ...
a symmetrical cylindrical form or any ...
fitted into the closed ends of the uprights thus.

This form of construction seems to ... itself
particularly to the ... construction
everywhere, though scarce but as would be
chosen by one of our Carpenters. The uprights

Are they about eighteen feet high, with a diameter
of about three feet or it is big. When we become
acquainted with the fact that a regular log is
laid at the section of the ... that it can account
for the movement without machinery. ... such
large logs. The he is accompanied by a distribution
of ... as the party the man for whom the ...
is being built, well known on the west coast by
the Chinook name Potlatch. Such a ... as

this accommodate several families is one acre
of the town, each occupying a certain corner or
portion of the interior.

In west return, however, to the canoe both which
constitute the most distinctive feature of Haida
village. To make one of these a large sound cedar
tree, probably three or four feet in diameter, is
chosen. Somewhere 20 yards from the waters edge,
felled, trimmed, of the wood down to the sea.
Being launched it is towed to the village site & is
hauled & canoe dragged up at or high water mark
on the beach. It is then shaped & carved. Some of
the Indians being famous for their skill in this
business & taking considerable time & practising
it. The log is hollowed behind into a trough, the

it. The log is hollowed behind like a trough, while it [light?], while the front is [carved?], [covered?] with a mass of grotesque figures in which the animal representing the totem or clan of the person to whom it is made takes a prominent place. It constitutes part of his [dwelling?], and may in some instances be fairly [described?]. When all is finished the post is taken to the place & firmly planted in the ground, to remain a thing of beauty till under the influence of the climate it becomes grey with age & hoary with moss & lichen.

The peculiar type [last?] most fully displayed on the carved posts is found more or less in all the [manufactures?] of the Haidas. The [skill to carve?] the [finest?] wooden [objects?], which [formerly?] served all [household?] purposes, [probably?] always [remained?]

peculiar animal form or grouping of forms more or less complicated or contorted. Though the artist may take to copy nature faithfully when he tries, as instanced in some of the masks used in dancing, it is not even proper to follow certain conventional ideas which affect a large urge to have become incorporated into the native mind.

of the art curves of the curtains of the theatres probably and some religious significance, and these connected with dancing ceremonies. It is reasonable to that most of these are said to have been derived from the Tshimsians of the neighbouring mainland, a people speaking a language quite distinct, of the within a few years formerly at ... war with the Haidas. The dancing ceremonies are divided, so far as I have been able to learn, into six classes, known respectively as Skā-ga, Ska-dal ...

Known respectively as _Ska-ga_, _Ska-dul_,
Kwai-o-guns-o-lung, _Ka-ta-Ka-gun_, _Ska-dut_
& _Hi-att._

It there I have been fortunate enough to see one,
the _Kwai-o-guns-o-lung_, a discipline which
serves ready as illustration of the time I may
some to illustrate a class of ceremonies once
common among the Indian peoples, but which have
for almost everywhere passed away.

Standing after dark from our boat out — the southern
end of the pier sandy beach on which Skidgate
village stands, we form the... that
quite arrested, but could discern a dim glare of
light at a distance, a distinguish the tumultuous

Sound of the alarm. Scrambling as best we might
in the dark & the mud which Big Boys along the
front of the row of houses & burrowing & scraping felt
our various obstacles, we reached the front in which
the alarm was going on. The door was but a slit in
the side of the ... middle of the front, a slit but open
through the hut, the canvas for ... a ... of the
... cast the ... fashioned buildings. Pushing
it open, the door(?) a glare of light flashed out, what had
journeys been seen and so it filtered through the
various crevices of the hut, a lantern, in fact
... behind & among the dancers who
stood within the hut, with their backs to the front
wall. Edging through them we crossed the open
space in which the fire — well supplied with

space in which the fire — will supplied with ammunitions logs — was burning, a seated onlookers on the floor considered a crowd of onlookers at the further end. The hour was of the unobbling shops, but was all except in the centre as placed the case, statues bound with the ground outside. The floor area carved with cedar planks with the exception of a square space in the centre for the fire, of the food & chattels of the family soon piled here & there in heaps along the walls, leaving the greater part of the interior clear.

The houses, as already stated, occupied the front row of the building while the audience disposed themselves along the sides & at the further end, many filling themselves around the space, squatting in various attitude on the floor, or curious by-

Even women & children [of] all ages. The danger of the
fire [escaping] by similar openings in the roof without
causing any inconvenience as its glare [lights]
illuminates the [front] 2 [rooms] full [front]. The
Japanese, in the [distance] about twenty in number,
were dressed according to [their uniform plan], but
attired in their best clothes — or at least their
best — strong ones — and the addition of certain
ornaments & badges appropriate to the occasion.
All, or nearly all, wore head-dresses [forming]
constructed, twisted cedar bark & ornamental
[and Pearls], or, as in one case, with a [wreath]
circle of the whiskers of the sea-lion. Children
girdles made of cedar bark, formed as

girdles made of cedar bark covered an
ornamented front tassels were very numerous.
The men wore ... covered with fringes of
... bark string strung together which rattled as
he moved. Many of them held sprays of fresh
spruce in the hand, & were covered about the
head with downy feathers, which also floated
in abundance in the warm air of the ... house.
Some had rattles & added to the din by shaking
these ... at the accustomed part of the
song. Five women took part in the dance,
standing in front in a row & were served
but few ... , served having the
peculiar valuable cedar-bark & foots-wool
shawls made by the Tsimsians, the head -
dresses of the women were all alike, consisting

in each. Carve of a small crook or semblance of a face. Carved mother's work, & inlaid with pearl, haliotis shell. These attached to a cedar bark serration & built — covered with gay feathers & tassels, stood before the forehead, while at the back in four canes, depended a train with ermine skins. The faces of the men & women topped in the dance were gaily painted, vermilion being the favourite colour.

The man, always as master of the ceremonies, stood in the middle of the track now of proprietors slightly higher than the rest. He was dressed almost altogether in white & held in his hand a long wand with which he kept time & cut off the singing. A second man held a white stick with a altogether in white & held in his hand a long wand with which he kept time & beat off the singing.

A second man held a white-stick with a slit & trimmed feathers at the top. He occupied a prominent place at one side, in the front-row of dancers! & seemed to speak in a recitative voice at times when the others would for utterance to monosyllabic sounds.

The performer on the drum — a flat tambourine-like article formed of hide stretched on a hoop sat opposite the dancers & near the fire, so that they could modulate [?] See each others movements. The drum was beaten on regularly with double knocks, thus — tum tum — tum tum — tum tum — tum tum — *

but the sound the dancers kept-time in a sort of chant or song to which words are set, & which swells into a full chorus or dies away according to the emotions of the dancers

the Castanetas, who twirls marking time through
then stopping a few words of adieu then an
exportation. To the drumming & singing the
dancing also keeps time, following it to try dance.
Always has a spasmodic twitch frame though
the crowd of dancers, who scarcely raise their feet
from the floor between by double jerks, shuffling
the feet a little out the same time. Those who dance
hat — Expressing the women before referred to —
turn about they move in three or four jerks &
then turn back again in the next three or four ..
These women also allow their heads to throw as
though loosely supported on pivots, bending identically
as they shuffle about. When the Chorus swells to

as they shuffle about. When the Chorus swells to
forte, the rattles are plied with the fullest zest
& the din becomes very great. After the performance
has continued for ten minutes or so the theatre

The Ceremonies gives a sign & all winding
stop with a loud hugh! The dance is again
resumed by the perspiring Crowd at the signal
of the drum, which strikes up after a few moments
rest has been allowed.

The Crowd of ... paint to gaily smeared
forms of the ... light up the fire ... on the
while a rather ... & ... appearance, &
when excited in the dance the theatre may get
about ... give the grand old days to remain
when hundreds crowded the villages now occupied
by two, & nothing had eclipsed the grandeur
of their Ceremonies & doings.

of stories connected with localities, or accounting
for various circumstances, there are no doubt
very many among the Haidas. of the above ten
appended to collection. the fundamental narrative
of the origin I mean & the beginning of the present
state of affairs is the most important of their
myths. This is given below & I believe in
all its main points correct. That is to say unaltered
from its original traditional form. In most states
of meaning may in some cases be indistinct
has obtained through the medium of the Chinook,
rider of what little English my informant was
master of. —

How long ago there was a great flood by which all

For long ago there was a great flood by which all men & animals were destroyed, with the exception of a single Raven. This creature was very beautiful in an Indian bird, but — as with all animals in the old Indian stories — possessed the attributes of a human being to the greatest extent. His coat of feathers, for instance, could be put on or taken off, put on & off at will like a garment. It is even related in our version of the story, that he was born of a woman who had no husband, & that she made bows & arrows for him. And there, when old enough, he killed birds, & of their skins she sewed a cape or blanket. He thus were the little inner-bird with black head & neck, the large hawk & red woodpecker of the American woodpecker. The name of this being was Me-kil-etta.

When the flood had gone down Me-kil-etta

looked about, but could find neither his visitor companions
but a mate, & became very lonely. At last he
took a cockle shell from the track, & marrying it,
A constant ... to ... & thick harvests
of his ... for a companion. By & by in the
... to hear a very faint cry ... that of a newly
born child, but which gradually became louder,
the Atlantic little female child was seen, which
growing by degrees larger & larger was ...
... by the rivers, & from this union all the
Indians were produced & the country peopled.
The people, however, had many wants, & as yet
had neither fire, daylight, fresh water, or the
... fish. These things were all in the
possession of a great chief or deity, called

There once was a great chief or deity called Setlin-thli-pad, who lived where the Naase River now is. [Looters?] was first obtained by Ne-lil-stles in the following manner. The Chief had a daughter, & to her Ne-lil-stles covertly made love; & visited her many time unknown to her father. The girl began to love Ne-lil-stles very much & trust in him, while this was what he desired, & at length when he thought the time ripe, he asked on an occasion for a drink [wata?], saying that he was very thirsty. The girl brought him the water in the guthing upon buckets in common use, [but?] he drank off a little, & setting the bucket down beside him waited till the girl fell asleep. Then quietly drawing his cloak — matters, & lifting the bucket in his hand, he flew

out by the opening made for the smoke in the top
of the lodge. It was in great haste, flaring to the
followed by the people of the chief, & a little water
fell out here & there causing the numerous rivers
which are now found, between the Haida country
a few drops only fell, like rain, & so it is that
there are no large streams there to this day.

Ne-kil-stlas____ next wished to obtain fire, which
was alone in the possession of the Tsun Principal
being a chief. He did not dare, however, to appear
again in the chief's house, on account the chief's
daughter longer knew him found. Assuming
therefore the form of a single needle-like leaf of
the spruce tree he floated on the water near the

...the Sphinx tree. The floated on the water was the Frog, & when the girl — his former lover — came down to draw water, was Spied by her in the pond. She said. The girl carrying the water swallows without noticing it — the little leaf & shortly afterwards was a child who was so that, when the evening Pe-kli-stas, who had this again obtained an entry into the lodge. Watching his opportunity, he one day picked up a burning brand, & flying out as before by the smoke-hole — held at the top of the Lodge, carried it — away & spread fire everywhere.

All the time, however, the people were without daylight, & it was just the artifice of Pe-kli-stas to obtain this for them. This time & trick title another plan. He pretended that he also had light, & contrived to present it through the Chief denied

Some few childish stories serve to explain the origin of light & the praise of Osladen first.

the truth of this statement. It, however, is some way inside an object-teaching a resemblance to the moon, which, while all the people were out fishing on the sea in the perpetual night, he allowed the ... seen from under his cloud of feathers. It cast a faint fullness across the underside of the

people & little-kingdom though was caused by a twilight moon. Disfeatured finding he was on the sole journey of light & losing all concept of his prophecy, the great chief immediately placed the sun & moon where we now see them.

One thing more, much depend still remained in the possession of Setta-ki-jod — the totaller, a little pile high forged of the fabulous fire, part-world contras a source of stable oil. Now

Koit-woot-Coutan a source of valuable old. Now the Shog was a friend an occupation of the Chief & had access to his property, including his slave & attackers. Ne-kil-stlas entured that the Sea-gull & the Shog should quarrel, by telling each that the other had spoken evil of him. At last he set them together, when, after an angry conversation, they followed his advice & began to fight. Ne-kil-stlas knew that they two men attacker in his stomach, & so urged the combatants to fight hard & to lie on their backs & strike out with their feet. This they did & finally the Shog threw up the attacker, which Ne-kil-stlas immediately seized. Turning a canoe from a rotten log, he lowered it & Quincey wist the scales of the attacker, & then coming at my bit near the great Chief's lodge

24

Said that he was too cold & worked & time in a
warm himself, as he had been working a great
catch of Potlatches which he had left somewhere
not far off. Setters-he-girls said that this could
not be true as to any Potlatches the girl, but Potlatches
invited the chief to take off his clothes & at his count.
Finding him turned with scales the chief became
convinced that Potlatches inside there which he had
must exist, & gave in dispute at finding to
had up the monopoly, & turned all the Potlatches
loose, saying, at the same time, that every year they
would come in vast numbers & continue to bow
his liberality & be a monument to him. This they
has never failed to do since that time.

among the Tsim-su, recomanies of existence,
such as light, water & fire.

The Het-stlas of the Haidas is equivalent in
function & scene to the Us-tas of the Carrier Tinneh.
Us-tas are almost endless series of prologue
& often disgusting adventures are related, &
analogous tales are related about the Het-stlas.

One of these tales tells that having disguised himself
as a dead woman, & floating upon the surface of the
sea, it was swallowed by a whale, which, by
violent pains being thus induced to strand
himself became a prey to the Haidas, himself
the Het-stlas meanwhile walking untroubled
telly at the proper moment.

→ Such details as these others from concerning the
habits, customs & thoughts of a people semi-barbarous,

The Collection →
similar to

The Collection & Study of

Such details as these concerning the habits, customs & thoughts of a people semi-barbarous, & who appearing have been before our eyes in the universal crumbling of civilization, may seem to be of little importance. They lead, however, into a wider & interesting region of speculation, embracing the question of the origin & interrelation of the American aborigines, their wanderings, & all the unwritten pages of their history which we can hope to learn — the most careful enquiry, and in due outline, but are led to task ourselves in particular in regard to whether too has the origin of the language through conventionalized art which exhibits itself in many of the works of these people, the social customs, which until a human almost as strong as that of fashion among ourselves.

causes them to dwell on their time to
ceremonies apparently meaning less but which
serve to form the bonds & keep working
of society among them. Here they can think of
a people who —

"Trying, found shelter in the Fortunate Isles,
and kept their usages, their arts & laws.
To disappear of a slow gradual death
to dwindle & to perish one by one —
Strewn in their narrow tombs."

as have they been developed slowly in a community
separated from the human stock a very long
period of night — had they been brought
face to face with a superior power — they found in
the course of ages into an independent civilization.

the course lays out an undoubted civilization.

the best of Mexico or Peru? Or even the

to answer such questions fully, but in regard

to these people of the North-West Coast we turn

that there are several several instances in

which Japanese junks, driven by the prevailing

winds & currents, far have carried across

the whole breadth of the North Pacific, and that

the voyage across Behring's Strait—to the

North is short, & to Iona occasion also on the

present-day made on the winter is by the beginners.

It is therefore more improbable that people

with their race onto Ing from here to

time for has home to the western coast

of America, & that it is to eastern Asia

that we must look for the origin of its peoples.

27

One question at least of a practical character
must be answered for the Haidas & other surviving
civilized tribes of the North-West Coast. What is to
be done with them? It is probable that they have already
nearly reached that critical point of the final
contact with the whites, beyond which they cease to
diminish, & may begin to increase in numbers.
It would be a mistake to attempt to bring these
people back into a state of tutelage such as
that which we found them in, keeping some of our
Indian tribes in a condition nearly stationary,
without regard to civilization, for a period from a
two hundred years. They do not require reserves

two hundred years. They are not again owners of water land, for though having strict ideas of their proprietary rights in their native islands they are essentially fishermen. Some consider arrangement must, in the frontier... to come to for the canal, while the people are taught future their first instinct a way that it will leave a fundamental value unlike to become artisans — for in handicrafts the Haidas show a special aptitude — & encouraged to become sailors. —

George M. Dawson.

References

The Haidas original notebook can be viewed at: McGill University Archives, Montreal, Quebec, Dawson-Harrington fond MG 1022.
https://digitalarchives.library.mcgill.ca/MUA/MG1022/series6/mua dawson fonds MUAMG1022-6-104.pdf

About 70% of the essay, slightly edited, appeared in **Harper's New Monthly Magazine.** 1882, "The Haidas" by George Mercer Dawson. P. [401]-408 : ill. EN ISBN: 0665148577, 9780665148576. The CIHM/ICMH Microfiche can be viewed at:
https://ia600208.us.archive.org/31/items/cihm 14857/cihm 14857.pdf

Report on the Queen Charlotte Islands.
Author George M Dawson 1849-1901.
Print Book 1880 Montreal : Geological Survey of Canada, ISBN: 9780665036569, 0665036566
OCLC Number/Unique Identifier: 606215347
https://bac-lac.on.worldcat.org/oclc/606215347?lang=en
and
https://open.library.ubc.ca/collections/bcbooks/items/1.0222501
Physical Description:
v, 239B pages, 14 leaves of plates
Three folded maps inserted. With appendices:

    APPENDIX A.
        ON THE HAIDA INDIANS OF THE QUEEN CHARLOTTE ISLANDS.
        Physical peculiarities and dress
        Food
        Social organization
        Religion and medicine
        Potlach, or distribution of property
        Dancing ceremonies
        Social customs
        Arts and architecture
        Traditions and folk-lore
        First contact with Europeans—Fur trade
        Villages
        Population

    APPENDIX B.
        VOCABULARY OF THE HAIDA INDIANS

    Appendix A & B can also be viewed at:
    https://www.canadiana.ca/view/oocihm.14877/3

A separate notebook by GMD written during his 1878 survey of the Queen Charlotte Islands, including sketches, can be viewed at:
https://digitalarchives.library.mcgill.ca/MUA/MG1022/mua george-mercer-dawson-diary 1878 envelope-49 MG1022.pdf